Patricia Moffett

AG 2 4 '21

Cut It!

15 Fun
Papercutting Projects
for Kids

SCHIFFER
PUBLISHING

4880 Lower Valley Road · Atglen, PA 19310

Produced by BlueRed Press Ltd, 2020
Designed by Insight Design Concepts Ltd.
Type set in Neutra Text and Grilled Cheese

ISBN: 978-0-7643-6066-4
Printed in Malaysia

Published by Schiffer Publishing, Ltd.
4880 Lower Valley Road
Atglen, PA 19310
Phone: (610) 593-1777; Fax: (610) 593-2002
Email: Info@schifferbooks.com
Web: www.schifferbooks.com

For our complete selection of fine books on this and related subjects, please visit our website at www.schifferbooks.com. You may also write for a free catalog.

Schiffer Publishing's titles are available at special discounts for bulk purchases for sales promotions or premiums. Special editions, including personalized covers, corporate imprints, and excerpts, can be created in large quantities for special needs. For more information, contact the publisher.

We are always looking for people to write books on new and related subjects. If you have an idea for a book, please contact us at proposals@schifferbooks.com.

contents

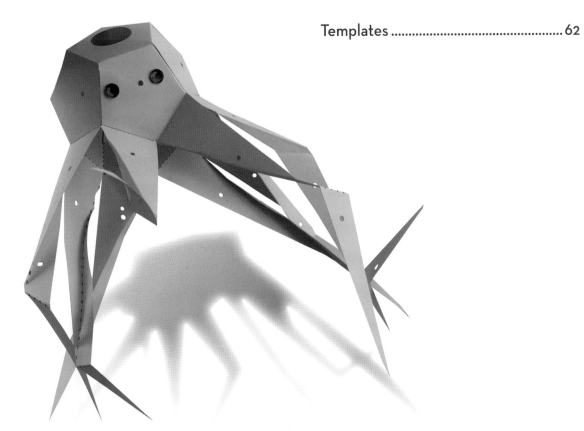

Introduction

Welcome to Cut It!

Each of the fifteen projects in this book are based on a tale, or set the scene for one to be told.

In making the pieces you'll work through many papercutting and folding techniques. You'll be exploring quilling in the Green Man Stained-Glass Window, geometric paper sculpture in the Kraken Lampshade, and curling and fan folds in the various masks, as well as the effects of cutting through folded paper when making **papel picado** (perforated paper) for the Mexican Halloween Bunting.

These paper projects come to life in the "Moving Parts" section, where you'll be adding animated elements—some with built-in lighting!

I hope these projects will inspire you to think of lots of new ideas for papercutting and make you want to design your very own paper pieces once you have mastered the various techniques and tricks.

Paper Playground

Papercutting Basics

There are many wonderful shapes to be made by simply cutting, bending, and shaping paper. The way you cut paper—whether you snip it or tear it—and the directions you fold it make it bendy or stiff. Think of this as sculpting with paper and card.

Here are some of the basic forms to get you started:

Zigzags and Folds

Fold a strip of paper to make a zigzag.
Pinch one end of it—see how strong it has become.
What could it be . . . a wing? a fan?
We'll be using this fan shape in two of the projects in the book—can you find them both?

When it's folded into a long strip, the zigzag is very bendy. You can fold two zigzags together to make a flexible strip—can you find where we've done that in our projects?

If you cut holes in the fold, you get lovely repeating patterns. We've folded paper in other ways before cutting holes in the Mexican Halloween Bunting—check it out!

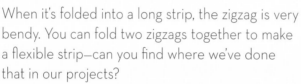

These fans were made from parts of a circle.

Punched Shapes

Punching holes in paper can be useful and decorative. Sometimes we need holes to thread string through, as for the Venetian and Neptune Masks. Other times the holes are simply for decoration, as shown off by the Kraken Lampshade.

Keep the punched-out holes themselves, since they make handy decorations.

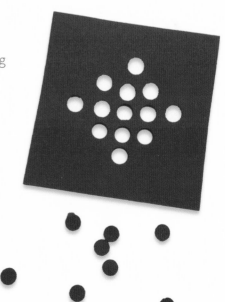

Pick up a sheet and play with it. Try different thicknesses and textures of paper. See how shiny paper reflects the light when folded.

Informal Shapes

Rolling

Rolling pieces of paper can add texture and height to a project. From a distance, the pieces of rolled paper can look like flowers—look at the texture that tissue paper gives when cut and rolled in the Sleeping Beauty Mint Tin Diorama.

Curls

Paper curls can be made by stretching one side of the piece along a ruler. Can you spot how these have been used in the Neptune Mask project?

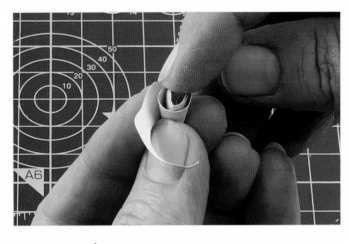

Paper Weight

Paper comes in many different sizes and thicknesses. All the projects in this book use standard letter-size 20 lb. paper (8.5 x 11 in. / 216 x 279 mm). In some places the paper has to be thicker, and different weights are shown. Craft stores will be able to provide this.

Cut Fringe

You can make a fringe by cutting into or tearing the paper. Of course the torn edge will look fuzzy, and the cut one sharp—it depends on the type of effect you'd like to make. Both types can then have a curl added by running scissors or a ruler down one side.

The direction you make cuts doesn't have to be at right angles to the edge of the shape.

Sometimes the decision between tearing and cutting depends on the type of paper you are using. In the Venetian Mask project, a torn fringe would have looked good for the feathers, but using crepe paper makes this very difficult.

The fringes here look best cut at an angle.

Working with the Templates

Copying the Templates

The templates at the end of this book can be traced or scanned, then printed onto your chosen paper.

Scanning

The easiest way to get the templates onto your paper is to scan them straight from this book. We have designed the book with enough space so that you can get all the image onto your scanner without damaging the book itself. You may have to turn the book upside down sometimes, but it will work.

Scanning also lets you scale the templates up or down to make the finished objects bigger or smaller. Once you have a scan of the template, it can be printed straight onto your chosen paper.

Tracing

If you don't have a scanner, you can trace the templates straight onto 80-grams-per-square-meter (gsm) paper (the usual paper used in a printer). You will then have a set of patterns to cut around.

Making Patterns

You can trace around the pattern onto your chosen paper and then cut it out, or you can cut straight around the pattern itself. If you want, you can use clips or pegs to keep the pattern next to your paper, especially when the card you're cutting is nearly done.

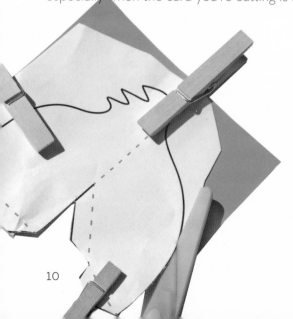

Cutting

Using Scissors

For nearly all the projects in this book, special scissors—called decoupage scissors—are the best. These make precise cuts that are easy to control by squeezing the handle together. It's really worth getting a pair, but if you can't find them, then ordinary scissors will do the job.

You hold a pair of scissors in one hand and use your free hand to help guide the paper. When cutting curves, use your free hand to turn the paper into the scissors,. Practice doing this instead of turning the scissors. It really helps make smooth curves and stops the paper bunching up in the blades.

> **Tip:**
> Turn the paper toward the scissors as you cut.

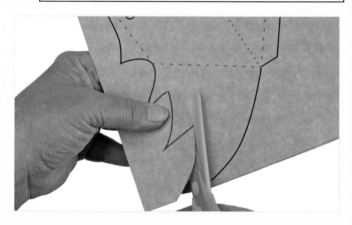

Cut all the lines that go in the same direction at the same time. Then turn the paper and cut lines that go another way. This method gives crisper cuts and stops the paper from crumpling and jamming.

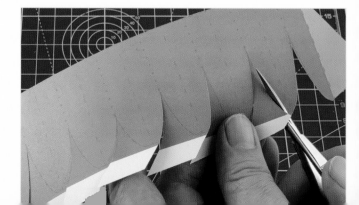

Cutting Windows

When you need to cut a window out of a piece of paper, you can start this off by folding the sheet gently, by making a starting snip. Then, poke your scissors through the starting snip to cut the window.

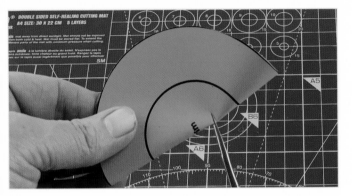

Cutting a window out of thick card is trickier since you can't bend the card to make your starting snip. Instead, try using a hole punch to make a hole that you can poke your scissors through. You'll need to make several holes close together.

Another option is to ask an adult to start the windows for you, or to cut them out with a craft knife.

Fancy Cuts

You can find decorative-edge safety scissors in hobby and craft stores. They give lovely detail with every cut. Try mixing up different styles for varied effects.

Scoring

It's easier to fold paper and card if it's been scored first.

Scoring is when you run an empty pen or a scoring tool along the crease to be folded before attempting the fold itself. Place a ruler next to the line you need to score so that the tip of the tool rests on the line. Pressing quite firmly, run the tool up and down the ruler for the length of the line. A small snip at both ends of the line to be folded will also make things easier and help the fold.

Mountain and Valley Folds

This book uses mountain and valley folds on the templates. A mountain fold is shaped like the top of a mountain, with the fold pointing upward—this is shown with a blue dotted line. A valley fold is shaped like a valley, with the fold pointing downward—this is shown by a green dotted line.

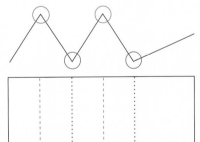

-------- Mountain

·········· Valley

1. Red Riding Hood Lantern

Materials

2 letter-sized sheets of 32 lb.
  paper, in white or cream
Battery-powered night light
Scissors
Stick glue

This pretty lantern has a scary surprise when lit up. Putting a night light inside the cottage turns grandma into the wolf!

Little Red Riding Hood likes to travel deep into the woods to bring her grandmother something nice to eat. It's a dangerous place, but she should be OK if she sticks to the path. But there's a Big Bad Wolf in the woods, and he's taken the place of her grandmother in her bed. Things don't look good for Little Red Riding Hood.

How will she know that things are not as they should be?
Warn her! Switch on this light to reveal that grandma is really a wolf!

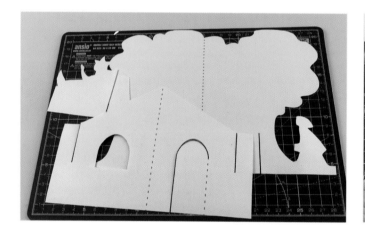

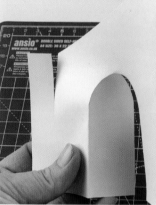

1 Scan and print, (or trace and cut out) the three parts of the lantern on pages 62 and 63. Fold the mountain and valley folds as shown by the green and blue lines.

2 Glue the wolf **A** behind the window **B** so that only the grandma part shows.

3 Attach the front **B** to the back **C**, using the slots.

4 Place over a battery night light. In a dark room, turn the light on and watch grandma turn into the wolf!

2. Green Man Stained-Glass Window

The ancient green man of medieval legend has a face made out of leaves. He is a nature spirit, and versions of him appear all over the world. Why not hang him in your window in the winter as a reminder that spring will soon return and that leaves reappear on the trees?

Why not use this method to make other designs? There are lots of stories and myths involving plants that could give you ideas for similar projects. The method shown here can be used to make another design based on anything you can think of.

Materials
About 4 toilet paper tubes
Black acrylic paint or spray paint
Black rollerball pen
Colored tissue paper
Glue pen
Ruler (ideally metal)
Shallow cake tin or lid

1 Flatten a toilet roll tube and draw across it lines the same width apart. I have used 0.25 in. (1 cm) spacing.

2 Cut the lines into strips.

3 Practice making shapes out of the strips. You can use them whole, cut them into pieces, then curl the strips to make different shapes.

4 Start to plan your design by placing the shapes into the cake tin or lid. The tin will hold the design in shape.

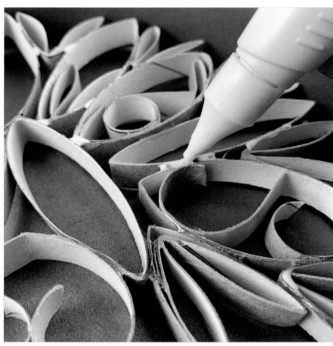

5 The curves of the strips act like springs and press against each other. There'll be a point where you can feel that the design is full when it starts to become firm.

6 Add dabs of glue with a glue pen where the strips touch each other. Keep turning the design to check that you've covered all these places. Glue all the pieces where they touch. Leave it to dry.

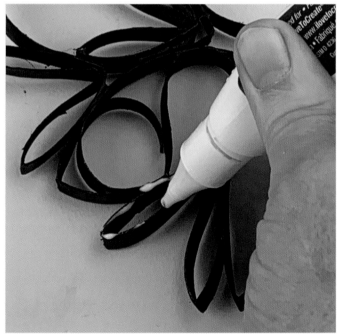

7 Once it's dry, the design can by tipped out of the cake tin or lid. Spray-paint it black and leave it to dry again.

8 When the paint is dry, decide which is the front and which the back of the model. Working on the back, pick a shape and choose a color of tissue paper for it. Go around the edge of the shape with the glue pen.

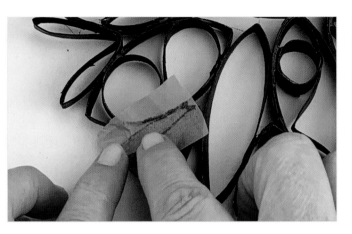

9 Place the tissue paper over the glued shape and press it down onto the glue. You will need to wait before working on areas next to each other until one of them is dry.

10 Once it is dry, neaten up each shape by snipping or tearing the tissue paper away very carefully.

11 Keep going by filling each space with the color you like. You can put more than one layer over some shapes and mix the colors.

12 Draw some detail on the back with pen or marker—but be very careful not to rip the tissue by pressing too hard.

13 Place the finished piece against the light so that the colors really glow.

3. Kraken Lampshade

Materials

3 sheets of 32 lb. colored paper
  for the size of one lampshade
Decoupage scissors
Hole punch
Stick glue
Stick-on gems for the eyes

The Kraken is a fearsome sea monster that looks like a giant octopus. Stories in the Norse sagas told that it lurked under the seas around Norway and Greenland, where it pulled ships down into the depths under the waves. Every Scandinavian sailor was afraid of the Kraken!

If you don't want to make a lampshade, you can cut the model without the top hole and make a mobile instead. Try making several in different colors and sizes, and out of different types of paper.

1 Cut out all the pieces along the red lines for parts **Ⓐ** and **Ⓑ**. Don't forget you will need two copies of the leg parts **Ⓑ**. Find the template on pages 64–65.

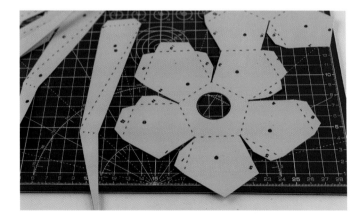

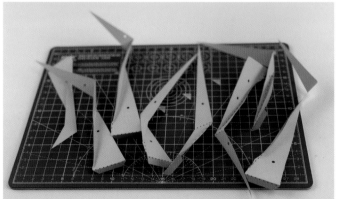

2 Punch some holes in each part, but don't go too close to the edges of the hexagons or the tabs will hide the holes.

3 Fold all the mountain and valley folds on the legs and put to one side.

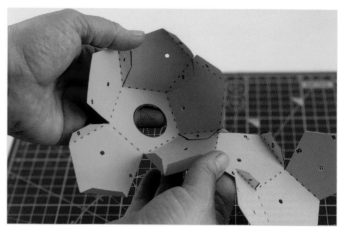

4 Fold all the valley folds on the head piece Ⓐ.

5 Find the tab and hexagon with 1 on it. Apply some glue to the tab and stick them together. Do the same for numbers 2 and 3. You will have something that looks like this.

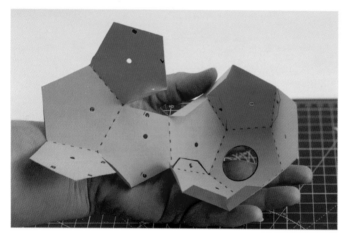

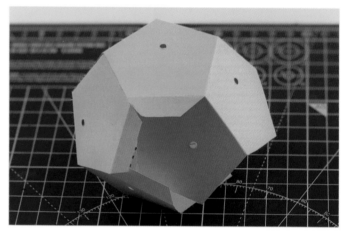

6 Doing the same for numbers 4 and 5 will complete that section.

7 Continue sticking down numbers 6 to 9 to nearly close the shape.

8 Numbers 10 to 12 can be stuck at the same time to complete the head.

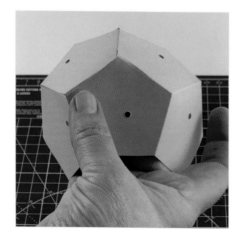

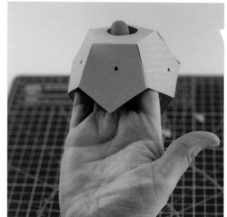

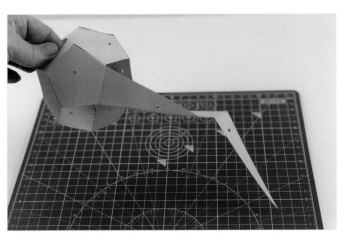

9 Stick a leg **B** by its tab onto one of the edges on the head.

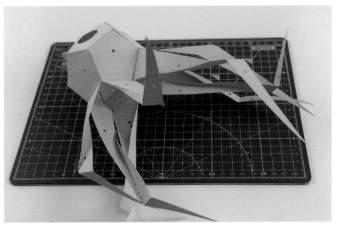

10 Continue doing the same for all eight legs.

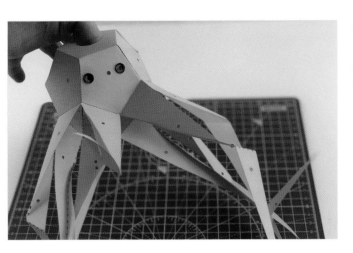

11 Find the hexagon between tabs 1 and 5. Stick some eyes on to give your Kraken a face.

12 Fit the shade over a LOW-WATTAGE bulb. This last bit is important, since a bulb that's too hot could scorch and even burn the paper.

4. Sleeping Beauty Mint Tin Diorama

A spell was cast on Sleeping Beauty and she fell asleep. She slept for so long that roses grew from the garden all around her.

Make this secret diorama inside a mint tin, using the technique of 3-D sculpture and paper rolling. Add as many flowers as you like— just make sure she isn't squashed when the lid closes!

Materials
1 mint tin measuring around 3.75 x 2.5 x 0.75 in. (9.5 x 6.2 x 2 cm)
Decoupage scissors
Fine marker
Glue dots
Stick glue

1 Take the marker and mark the middle point of all four sides of the bottom of the tin. Find template on page 66.

2 Place the tin over the gray block **B** with legs and move it about so that the halfway marks line up with the black dashes on the block.

3 Trace around the tin with a pencil and cut out block **B** just inside the pencil line.

4 Cut out **B**. Check the fit; you may have to keep cutting away, a sliver at a time, until the piece will fit in the bottom of the tin.

5 Cut out **D**. Take the top half of the body, bend the hair back, and glue the two tabs together. Make a fold at her waist where the tabs start to be fixed together.

6 Stick the tab to the base **B**, aligning the tab to the square area marked.

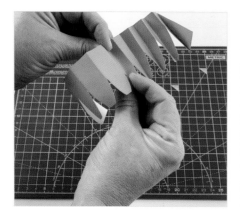

7 Cut out Ⓐ and fold the skirt. It's easier to fold all the dashed mountain folds first, then the valley folds.

8 Apply glue to the edge of the skirt folds on the back and the backs of the gray tabs.

9 Tucking her hands out of the way, glue the skirt over the base Ⓑ. Start by aligning the gray tabs to the edge of the base piece to help shape the skirt, then press the folds of the skirt down.

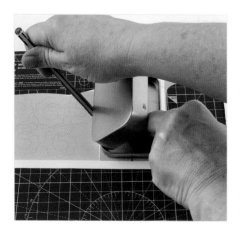

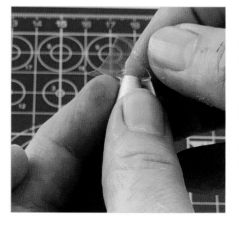

10 Place the tin lid over the gray block Ⓒ. Do the same as you did with the base Ⓑ in steps 2–4, and cut the piece to fit inside the lid. Place the base piece into the tin too.

11 Cut out the 3-D roses Ⓔ along the red lines and roll them to make flower shapes.

12 Apply a glue dot onto the base of a flower and then press it in to place over the white crosses.

13 There are white marks for four flowers to be placed. That will get you as far as this. Why not experiment and make many more flowers. Try using different kinds of paper and cover the lid too.

5. Paper Bag Forest

Materials

1 sheet of 32 lb. thin white
  card
Brown paper bag
Decoupage scissors
Hole punch
Pencil
Ruler
Small cutting mat or piece of
  cardboard
Stick glue

Here we have the perfect setting for many a fairy tale—what will yours be?
You could add a gingerbread house for Hansel and Gretel, as I have here,
or some tiny dolls for Snow White and the Seven Dwarfs ... or make up
your own story.

1 Keep the bag folded and turn it
so that the folded base is at the
back and you can see all of the
front face.

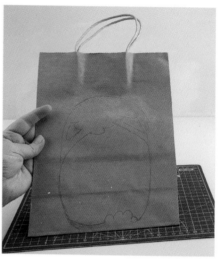

2 Draw out the front window. With
a pencil, sketch some tree shapes
on it like the ones in the picture
above.

3 Carefully poke the scissors
through, making sure your fingers
are out of the way. Cut out the
shapes of the trees.

4 You will now have a window in
the front of the bag.

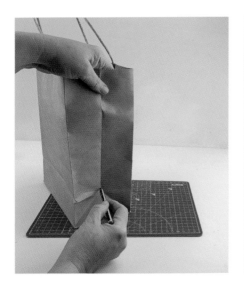

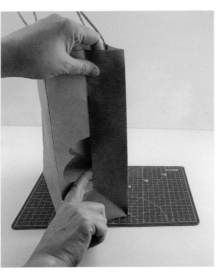

5 Make the bushes at the sides. Draw some leaves from the fold in the middle, toward the back of the bag.

6 Cut the line and push the shape inside the bag.

7 Your model will now look something like this. Notice how adding the bushes at the sides gives a sense of depth and size to the scene.

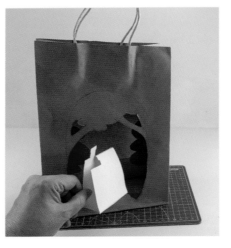

8 Scan and print, then cut out and fold the cottage **Ⓐ**. This folds very simply into a triangle shape and can be glued to the base of the bag. If you're feeling really creative, trace the dimensions of the model, but make your own design. I've added a tree—what else can you think of that would work well here?

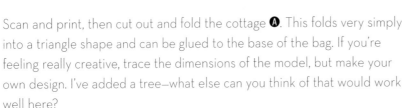

The basics of the scene are now finished, and it's time to add some special touches to tell a story.

Here, to get you started, the cottage model from page 67, along with a tree **Ⓑ**, have been added to make a Hansel and Gretel diorama.

Think about whether you want to leave the bag itself plain or add some decorative marker designs.

6. Cake Box Theater

Materials

1 small cardboard cake box
  6 x 6 in. (15 x 15 cm) and
  around 6 in. (15 cm) deep
All-purpose adhesive
Battery-operated LEDs
Card for the surround and
  scenery
Pens and markers to decorate
Stick glue
Scissors
Two wooden skewers

The early twentieth century saw a boom in theater building. Shows would include plays, musicals, and the new vaudeville variety programs. This tiny theater uses a flat-pack cake box as its structure. The holes in the sides allow actors to get on stage and move about.

Have you ever been to a theater performance? What kind of show would you put on if you were a director?

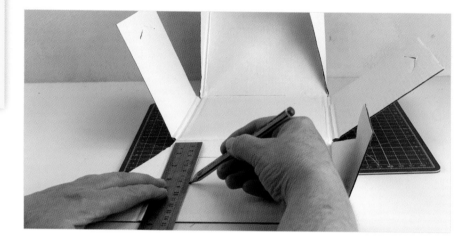

1 Look at the base of the cake box: two sides will have slots and two will have flaps. Draw your lines, then cut a block out of the sides with flaps. Leave at least 0.7 in. (2 cm) at the top, back, and base of each side.

2 Cut a window out of the lid, leaving a border of 0.25 in. (8 mm) around the sides.

3 Reassembling the box after making these cuts will give you the basics of the theater.

4 Scan and print out the templates onto the card of your choice for parts **A** to **D**. Cut around the gray lines. Color them in or decorate. Stick these parts on the front of the lid.

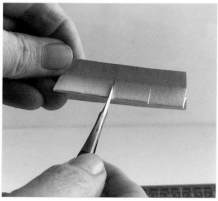

5 Attach the LED lights to a piece of paper, then glue the paper to the ceiling of the theater. The flex for the controls can be threaded through a slot.

6 Fold the mountain and valley folds of the scenery holders **E**. Snip grooves in the pointed part as shown.

7 Glue the scenery holders to the floor of the theater.

8 Cut out the scenery parts **F** (four pieces), and slot them into the scenery holders. When the scene is set how you want it arranged, place the lid on the box.

9 Glue wooden skewers onto the backs of pieces marked **G** (man, woman, sun, moon, clouds) so that they can be moved around the stage from the sides.

7. Postal Box Crankie

Materials

All-purpose adhesive

2 bamboo dowels, around
   0.25 in. (6 mm) diameter—
   longer than the height of
   your box

Battery-operated LEDs

1 cardboard box

2 clothespins

Decorative paper for
   covering the box

Electrical tape

Papers for the background
   scene

Pens, tissue paper, crayons

2 rigatoni pasta pieces

Ruler

A crankie is a moving panorama—in other words, moving pictures. An illustrated scroll is turned with handles (called cranks) to tell the tale, which can also be accompanied by words or songs.

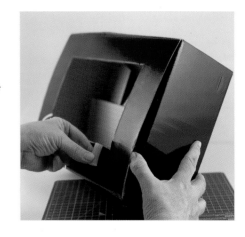

You can use any type of cardboard box, but ideally find one with a lid you can open and close. If the back is just slotted together, that's even better, since you can pass the switch for the LEDs through the slot, rather than have to make one. I've used a shoebox made from thin card.

1 Using the ruler, draw and cut out a window on the lid. Make the sides quite wide, since they have to hide the scrolls, and make sure that the bottom edge is deeper than the length of your pasta.

2 Decorate the outside of the box. I've used scrapbooking paper here.

3 With the battery and switch on the outside of the box, thread the LEDs into the box. If you don't have a box with a slot, you will have to make one.

4 Tape LEDs onto the back of the box, concentrating on the area you see through the window.

5 The position of the holes for the dowels should be inside the border of the frame and back from where the flap tucks in.

6 Start the hole off with decoupage scissors. Then wiggle a pencil in the hole until the dowel will fit through.

7 Push a dowel through one of the holes, then place a piece of pasta over the end of the dowel.

8 Push the dowel straight and down until it touches the bottom of the box. Glue the pasta piece in place.

9 When the glue is dry, support the pasta with a collar of sticking putty; repeat for the other side.

10 Glue a clothespin near the top of each piece of dowel and leave it aside to set properly.

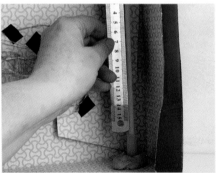

11 Now it's time for your story! Measure how high the window is, from just above it to the top of the pasta—this is the height of your scroll. Measure the window height within that, and make your pictures for this space.

12 Stick lots of pictures together to form a long strip. Don't be afraid to mix and match materials—use the switch between materials to good effect by changing the scenery with them.

13 Turn your story into a scroll but make sure you include a bit of extra background material at the start and end to stick around the dowel.

14 Tape the end side of the scroll to the dowel on the right, and wind the scroll onto that dowel.

15 Glue or tape the start of the scroll to the dowel on the left, and wind the story onto it to begin. Close the lid and turn the lights on for showtime!

Tips

- Experiment with the kinds of papers you use. Tyvek® gives a lovely texture, almost like Japanese paper. Smooth kitchen baking parchment has a lovely aged brown tone. Markers and black paper over tracing paper can give stained-glass effects. Whatever you use, make sure that the pieces are stuck together firmly. Here are some pictures using different materials.

White paper, with black paper cutout, and blue cellophane behind.

Black Tyvek with tracing paper and marker pen.

Black Tyvek on white Tyvek with marker pen.

8. Robot Puppet

It's now a hundred years since the word "robot" was used in a story. Robots have sparked the imagination, taking on roles both as our helpers and enemies here on Earth, and as explorers for other worlds. Who will your robot be? Friend or foe? What's their story?

When you're decorating your robot, don't be afraid to experiment and use cutout textures from magazines. Think about how their expression will work, and what things you can use to make those faces. Make more than one and swap around their features—imagine their stories and give each one a different personality and individual appearance.

Materials
2 thin, letter-sized sheets of 32 lb. card
1 letter-sized sheet of 60 lb. card
All-purpose adhesive
Hole punch
2 metal bottle caps from drinks bottles
5 paper fasteners with short tails
Scraps of colored or metallic paper
Wooden skewer

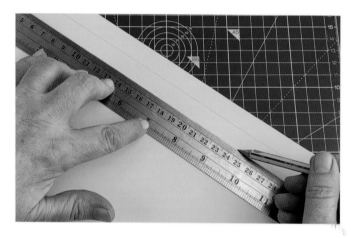

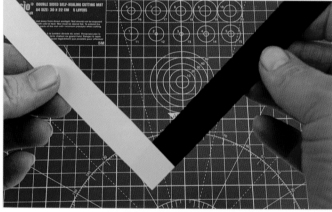

1 From the sheet of thin card, cut out 4 strips 0.5 in. (1.5 cm) wide, right down the long length of the A4 sheet.

2 Take two of the strips. Glue the end of one strip on top of the other at right angles.

3 Start to braid two strips together by folding the bottom strip over the top one at right angles. Repeat until you've used up the entire length of the strips. Glue the last two folds together. Repeat for the second two strips.

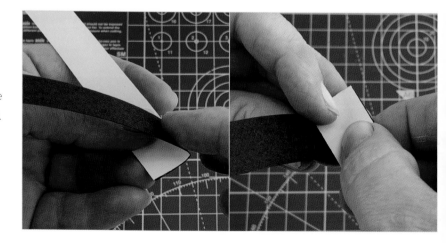

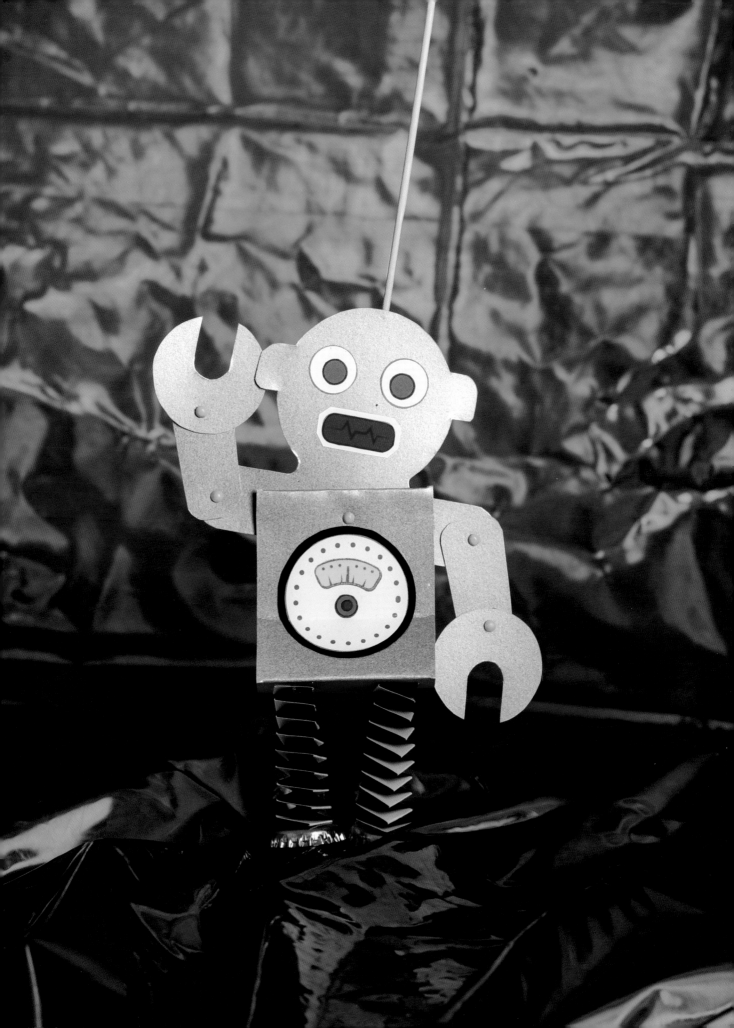

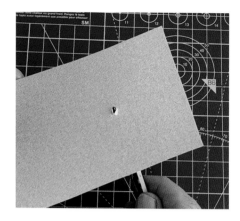
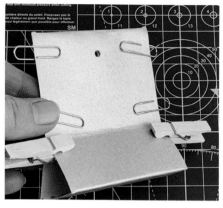

4 Trace the template (page 70) onto the reverse side of your paper and cut it out. With a hole punch or pencil, make holes where marked with a cross on the body, arms, and head pieces **A** to **D**.

5 Fold body piece **A**; hold it together with clips or pegs while the glue is drying. Decorate it when dry.

6 Stick one end of each plaited leg to a bottle cap, and the other end to the base of the body piece **A**. Press tightly until the glue has set.

7 Cut out the head **D**, arm **C**, and hand **B** pieces and decorate. Trace these gray shapes from the template on page 70 onto colored paper or make your own designs.

8 Attach all the pieces as shown, using paper fasteners. With the arm pieces, make sure you bend the fasteners close to the card, so that they are tight. This will help you pose the arms. Attach the head to the body with a paper fastener.

9 Glue the skewer onto the back of the head and make the robot walk by rotating from side to side to kick the legs forward. Tighten the paper fastener if the head moves too freely, to make walking the robot easier.

9. UV Cereal Box Tempest

Materials

4 letter-sized sheets of 60 lb.
  black card
All-purpose adhesive
Empty cereal box
Fat black marker
Fluorescent marker
Hole punch
4 paper fasteners with short
  tails
Scissors
UV LED lights
Wooden skewer

The most famous story about a tempest—which is a violent, windy storm—is a play written by William Shakespeare in about 1610. In the play, a magical storm is whipped up and wrecks a ship that was carrying a father and his baby daughter. They survive to live many years on a remote island.

The elements of this cereal box tempest are decorated with fluorescent marker, and the box is lit with UV LEDs.

1 Either trace or print the wave elements **A** to **C** from the templates on pages 72–73 onto black card (use a white or pale-yellow crayon). Otherwise, it should be possible to make out the black printing even on black card, so you can cut out the shapes.

2 Punch holes where the crosses are marked on the templates.

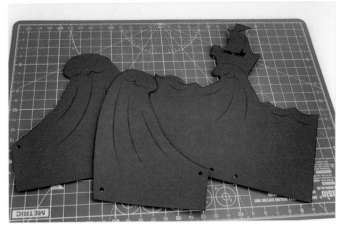

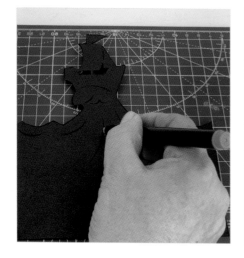

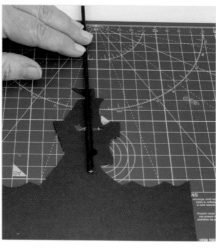

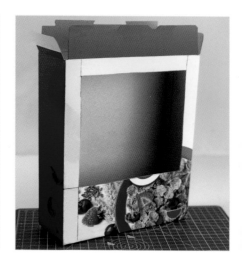

3 Draw some detail on the cutouts with the fluorescent marker. It looks really great if you draw over the edges with the marker.

4 Color the skewer with the black marker, then stick it to the back of the middle wave. Set it aside to dry.

5 Open up the top of the box and cut a hole in the front 6 in. (15 cm) wide by 5.75 in. (14.5 cm) high, and 2.75 in. (7 cm) from the base.

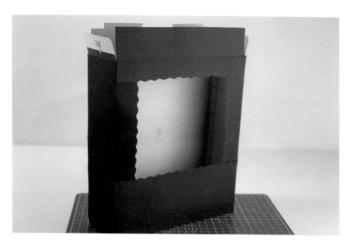

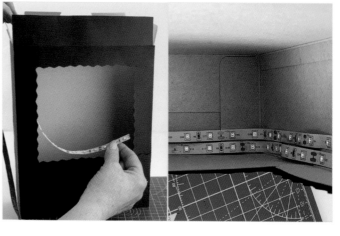

6 Cover around the window with strips that are slightly wider than the border you have left. Experiment with decorative scissors to make interesting edges.

7 Glue the LEDs inside the box, keeping them toward the front near the hole.

8 Cut out a sheet of black card to fit inside the back of the box. This is your backing card. With the marker, draw swirls over the card.

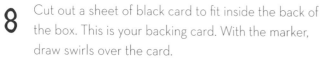

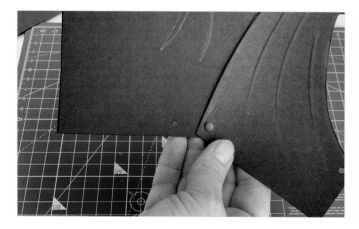 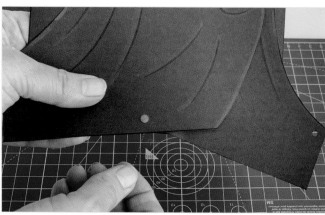

9 Attach piece **B** through the hole marked fastener 1, and connect it to the middle wave **A** through the hole for fastener 1, as marked on template **A**.

10 Attach part **C** through the hole marked fastener 2, and connect it to the middle wave **A** through the hole for fastener 2.

11 Center the fastened-together waves over the backing card. Line up all the pieces at the bottom edge. Punch holes onto the backing card through crosses marked on the right- and left-side waves.

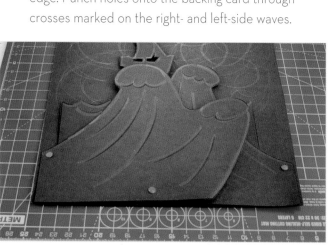

12 Fasten the waves onto the card with the remaining paper fasteners.

13 Glue the backing card to the back of the box. Turn on the lights! Move the stick up and down and left and right to animate the ship and waves. Now you have your very own Tempest!

10. A Wolf in Sheep's Clothing

Materials

2 letter-sized sheets of colored card

1 letter-sized sheet of white paper

All-purpose adhesive

Decoupage scissors

Paper clips or pegs

Pencil

Ribbon

The ancient Greeks told of a crafty wolf who dressed up as a sheep to trick the shepherd and the sheep in his flock. (The story didn't end well for the wolf!)

Play out this ancient tale as Ceri our model does on the next page with her sheep costume, or try telling some other wolf stories.

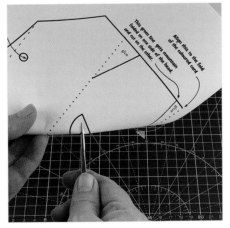
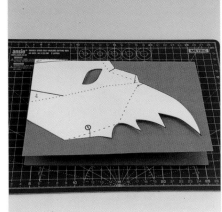
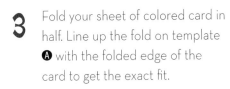

1 Trace or scan and print out the templates on pages 74–75 onto paper.

2 Cut out the eyehole by folding the paper to get the first snip in, then cutting around the eyehole. Continue to cut out along all the other red lines.

3 Fold your sheet of colored card in half. Line up the fold on template **A** with the folded edge of the card to get the exact fit.

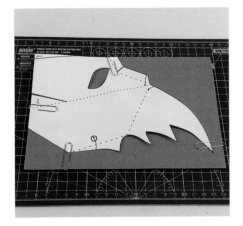
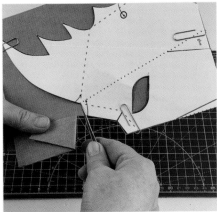
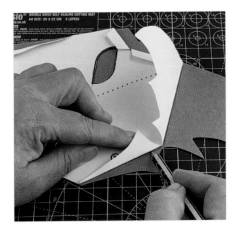

4 Clip the paper template to the card. Trace the eyehole with pencil. Cut around all the solid red lines. You will be cutting through both sides of the card.

5 Trace around the eyehole with a pencil. Cut out all around the paper, following the red lines. You'll need to move the position of the paper clips as you go.

6 Transfer the fold lines onto the mask by folding back the paper where you see a fold line. Draw along the fold with a pencil onto the mask.

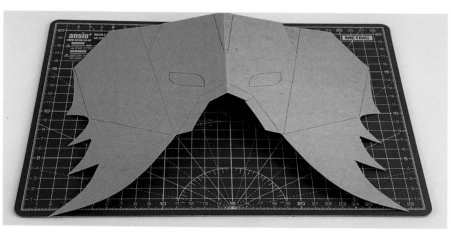

7 Flip the mask over. Trace the eyehole and fold lines to the other side.

8 Unfold the mask and your model should look like this.

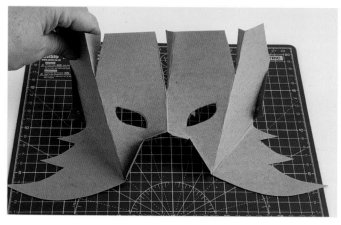

9 It's very important to note the lines in the middle above the eyes—the blue solid line on the template. One of these is a cut, and one a valley fold. Cut one side, then fold the other. Now cut out the eyes.

10 Fold all the other mountain and valley folds and you'll get to this point. Cut or punch out ribbon holes.

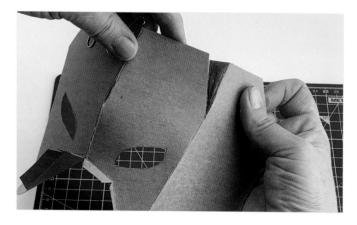

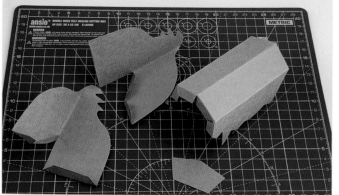

11 Glue the tabs along the top of the head and hold in place with paper clips until they are dry.

12 Cut out pieces **B** to **E** and trace onto your card, following steps 4-6 to transfer the design and cutout.

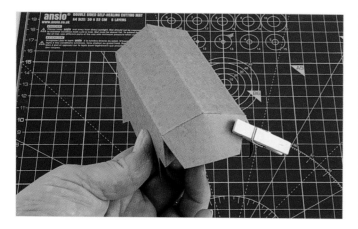

13 Fold the valley folds on the muzzle, then glue the nosepiece to it one tab at a time. Use pegs to hold things in place while the glue is setting.

14 When all the glue is completely dry, fold the earpieces and stick the tabs. Use paper clips or pegs to hold in place while the glue sets.

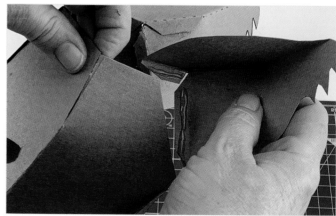

15 Stick the nose onto the face—this is quite tricky, and you'll need to ease it into place, then hold it with your hands while the glue sets. Be patient!

16 When the muzzle has set, stick the ears onto the head. Use pegs to hold them in position.

17 Thread ribbon through the holes and tie off. Your mask is now ready to wear. Where are those sheep?

11. Neptune Mask

Materials

3 sheets of letter-sized paper of different colors for the beard (I used blue papers in different shades and thickness)

2 strips of card, 1 x 8.25 in. (2 x 21 cm), for the strap

1 strip of shiny paper for the band

Ruler

Scissors

Stapler

Stick glue

Stick-on jewels

Neptune is the ancient Roman god of rivers and seas. Put this mask on and stare out at the waves ... enjoy the sound of the sea breezes rustling your ancient beard. Feel the power!

Paper curling is a really fun and effective way of sculpting paper, and by using a variety of papers you'll get an interesting and varied texture to the hair and beard. Explore the curling technique needed for this mask by experimenting with different types of paper—some curl more readily than others.

1 Scan and print out the design on paper and trace it onto your card.

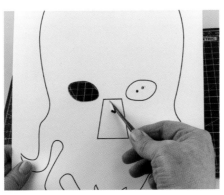

2 Start by cutting out the face piece.

3 Cut 14 strips of paper 1 inch wide from the three colors. Then cut these into three, stopping about 0.25 in. (1 cm) from the end.

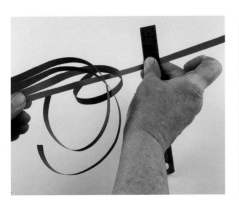

4 Curl the strips by holding one end and running the ruler along the paper.

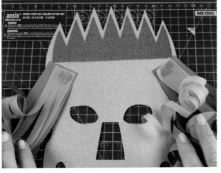

5 Stick the pointy part of the crown to the face piece. Under it, stick three bunches of curled paper on both sides, for his hair.

6 Glue the band across the top to hide the glued edges.

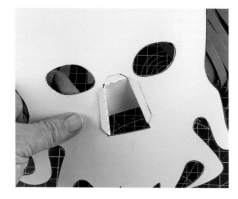

7 Fold the nose, then glue the tabs to the back of the face.

8 Glue the eyebrows and remaining beard curls onto the face. Then cover the stuck edges of the curls with the card beard pieces.

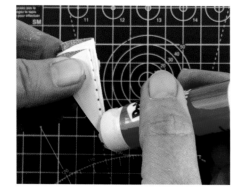

9 Cut and fold the shells. Run the glue along the creased folds at the back.

10 Glue the shells in place, along with any decorative gems.

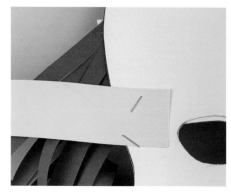

11 Staple each strap to the back of the mask and fasten these together to wear the mask.

12. Venetian Mask

Every year in Venice, there's a big carnival where people wear masks. Some of the most popular mask designs are characters from a set of plays known as the *Commedia dell'arte,* which dates from the sixteenth century and has been popular ever since.

This mask is based on the traditional Columbina style of half mask, but its fans and feathers give it an eighteenth-century feel. I have made my mask in gold and blue, but you can experiment with other color combinations.

Materials
Decorative-edge scissors and decoupage scissors
1 dowel, 0.2 in. (6 mm) diameter
1 gold paper plate, 9 in. (23 cm)
1 gold doily, 9.5 in. (24 cm)
1 gold doily, 7.5 in. (19 cm)
1 heavy crepe paper, 9.8 x 8.2 in. (25 x 21 cm), with the grain running along the long edge
Hole punch
Markers or stick-on jewels to decorate
Ruler
Tape glue, all-purpose adhesive, and stick glue

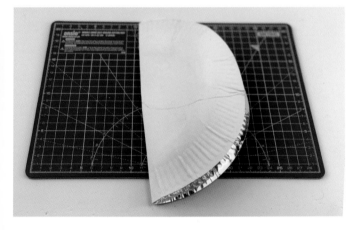

1 Fold the paper plate in half. Using the drawing below as a guide, draw a line for the notch of the nose and the eyehole.

2 Cut out the notch for the nose, using decorative-edge scissors. Then open up your plate and carefully cut out the eyepiece.

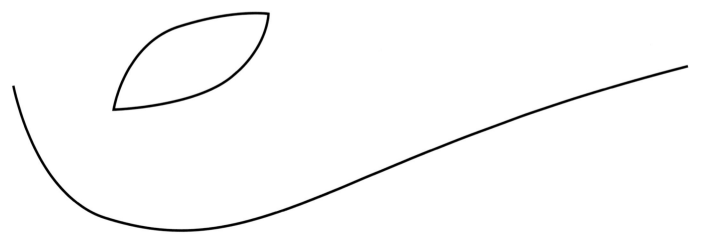

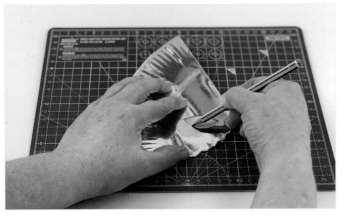

3 Refold your mask and use your first eye to mark the second eyehole, and then carefully cut it out.

4 Mark the center of the larger doily with a dot. Place the mask over the doily, then make a mark on either side where the mask touches the doily.

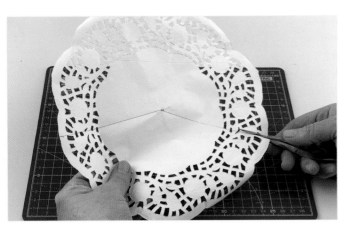

5 With a ruler and pen, join the marks on the edge with the dot in the middle, and cut along the lines.

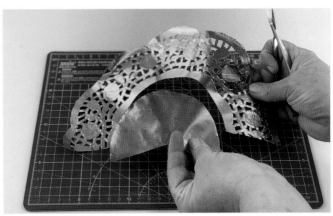

6 On the half that you measured against the mask, cut around between the lace border and the solid middle, with about a 5 mm margin.

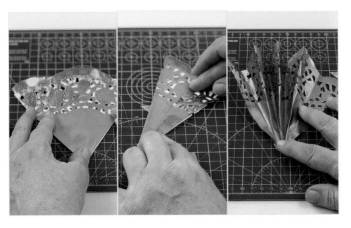

7 Fold the remaining piece to make a fan shape.

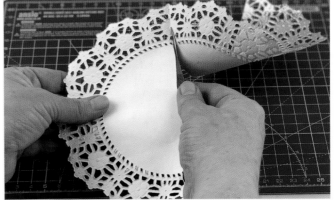

8 Fold the smaller doily in half and cut along the fold.

9 Glue half of the smaller doily on the back of the mask.

10 Cut out a 1.5 in. (4 cm) strip along the short edge of the crepe paper. The grain should be running parallel to the short edge of the strip.

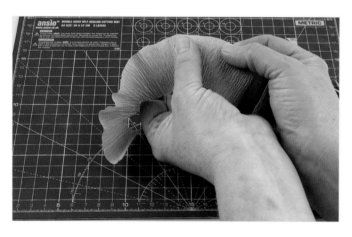

11 Gently stretch the first edge of the crepe paper to make a frill.

12 Glue the frill behind the smaller doily on the mask, pleating the crepe paper as you go.

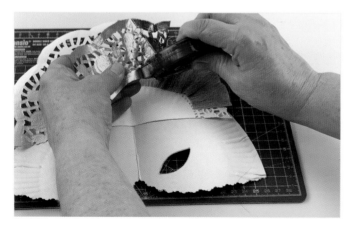

13 Then stick the remaining half of the larger doily behind that. Make sure they are all firmly attached to each other and won't flap or fall off.

14 Trim off the lace from the remaining part of the smaller doily. Look at the pattern and make mountain folds in the same place along the lace.

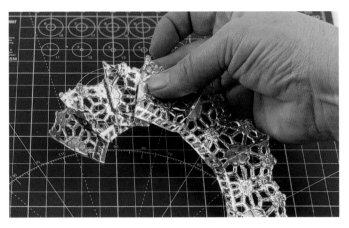

15 Bring the mountain folds across the center point between them—this will start to form a pretty curve.

16 Cut the remaining piece of crepe paper in two—making sure the grain runs along the long side—then trim each half into an oval shape.

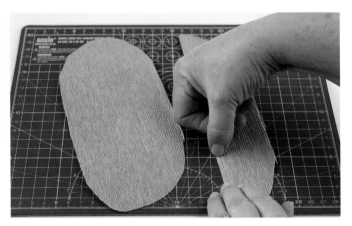

17 Fold each piece in half lengthwise and run your fingernail along the fold to make a sharp crease.

18 Make diagonal cuts from the edge, down toward the center, as close together as you can.

19 Run lots of stick glue along the folded edge of the fan (made in step 7).

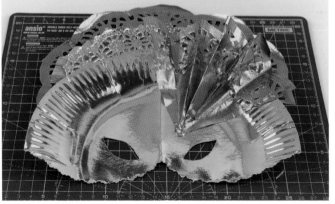

20 Stick the glued fan to the mask above one eye.

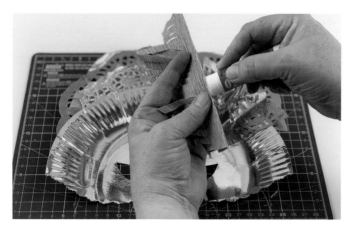

21 Run the stick glue down the spines of the two feathers, then stick them into the fan.

22 Glue the curved piece from step 15 in front of the feathers.

24 Glue the dowel to the back of the mask with the all-purpose adhesive. When this is dry, use the dowel to hold the mask in front of your face in true masquerade style.

23 Decorate with stick-on gems or markers.

13. Pirate Favor Boxes

Materials
1 letter-sized sheet of card per box
Decoupage scissors
Markers or crayons
Stick glue

Old-fashioned tales involving pirates such as *Peter Pan* and *Treasure Island* are thrilling stories of life on the wild ocean, with sea battles, coral reefs, and tropical islands—and the possibility of treasure for the taking.

So make your own treasure boxes! These little treasure chests make great place settings and favor boxes when stuffed full of booty for a pirate-themed party.

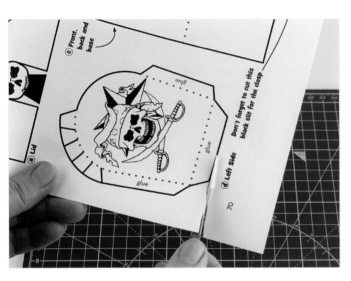

Scan the template on page 71 and print it out onto your choice of card, then cut around the red lines.

To make the instructions clearer, I've made the model on white paper without any decoration or color. If you have white crayons, why not try printing onto a dark card and make the highlights pop out.

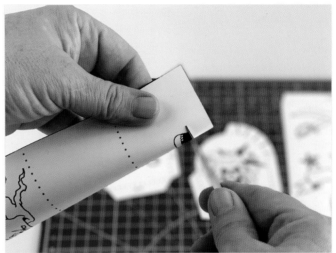

1 Cut a slit in the front of the box for the clasp. This is best done by folding the piece softly without making a crease, then snipping the fold.

2 Fold all the fold lines.

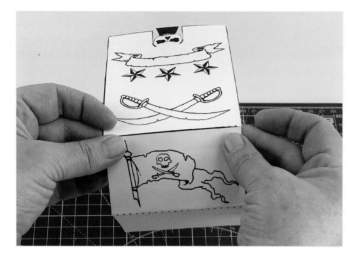

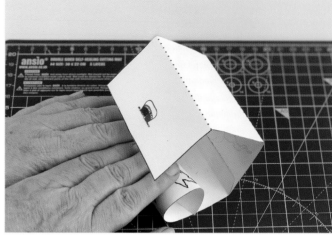

3 Glue the lid onto the back piece.

4 Gently roll the lid to get a barrel shape. This will help with fitting.

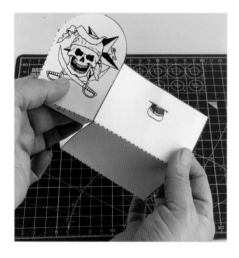

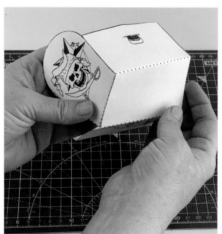

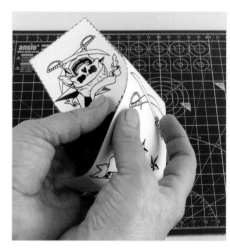

5 Glue one of the sides onto the already-glued-together lid and main piece. Glue in this order: front, base, back, and the tabs (the ones that will form the curve on the lid). Then repeat for the other side.

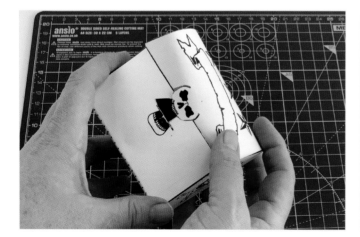

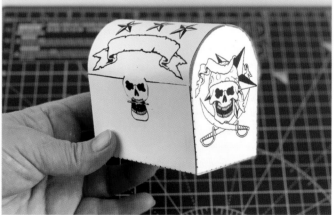

6 Tuck the large flaps on either side inside the chest, then the triangular piece into the slot.

7 The finished chest! Write the name of each guest in the banner—everybody will want one.

14. Mexican Halloween Bunting

The Day of the Dead is an important festival that takes place very close to Halloween. The idea that the spirit world and ours become joined is common to both.

Hanging rows of *papel picado*, or pecked paper, bunting is a popular way to decorate for the Day of the Dead, as well as many other fiestas.

The finished designs are glued onto string and strung from wall to wall. Use lots of rows to get the effect shown in the big picture.

Materials
Sheets of tissue paper in colors you like
Decoupage scissors
Length of string
Stick glue

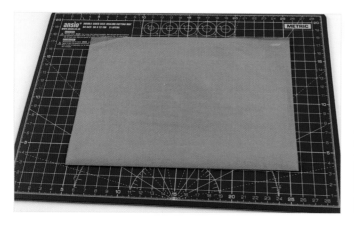

1 Fold a sheet of tissue paper in half.

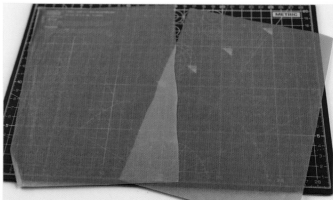

2 Cut along the fold to make two pieces. Use one of the halves for each cut.

Design A **1** Fold the paper twice, exactly as shown here.

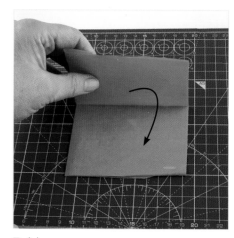

Fold 1

Fold 2

2 Cut out the design as shown here. It might help to trace the first one or two until you are really confident with your cutting.

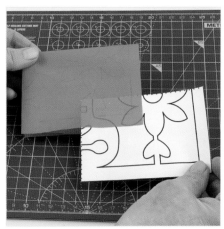

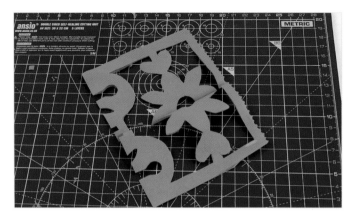

3 Carefully unfold the paper cut.

Try out some decorative scissors for frilly edges.

Design B

1 Fold the paper three times, exactly as shown here.

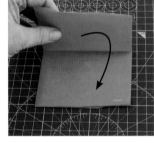

Fold 1   Fold 2   Fold 3

2 Cut out the design as shown here. It might help to trace the first one or two until you are confident.

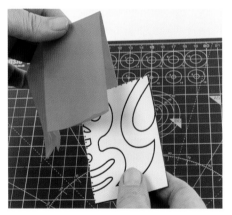

3 Unfold the design carefully. See the dancing skeletons!

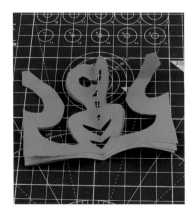
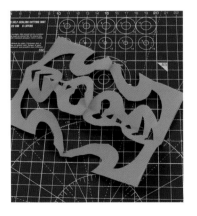
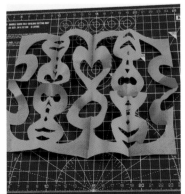

15. Mad Hatter Place Cards

Materials

1 letter-sized sheet of 32 lb. paper for each hat
Decoupage scissors
Pens or stickers to decorate
Stick glue

A crazy tea party was held in *Alice's Adventures in Wonderland*. It makes a great theme for a party—your guests could come as characters from the story, or you could just enjoy the mad hats.

These hats, with your guests' names on the ticket, make great place settings. You will need one piece of paper for each hat.

1 Scan and print out the templates onto colored paper—use a selection and swap the bands and base colors around for variety.

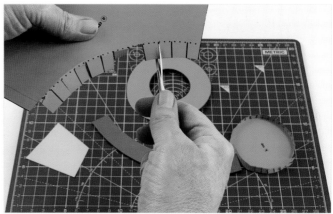

2 Cut out all the pieces and bend the tabs as directed.

3 If you're adding decoration, make sure to decorate the side that's not been printed on.

4 Curl the crown piece **A**, making sure the printed side faces inward, and glue the tab.

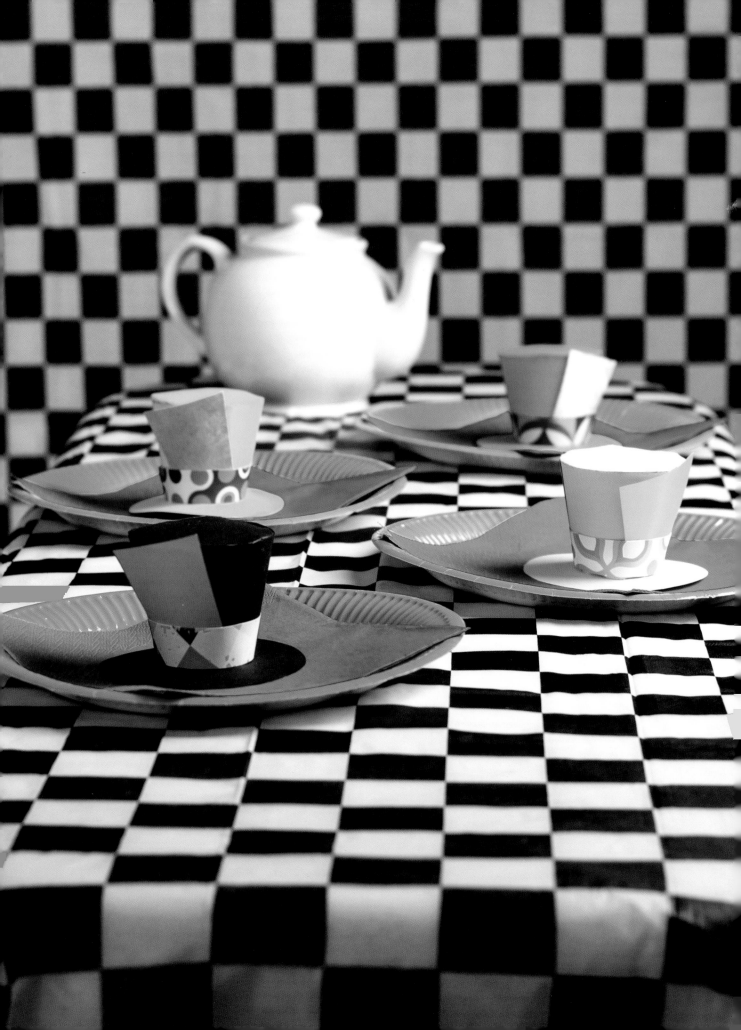

5 Apply glue to the tabs on the top piece **B**.

6 Carefully push the tabs inside the cone of the crown.

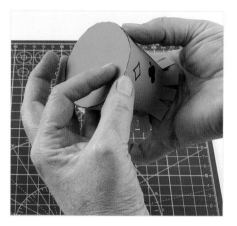

7 Put a hand inside and pinch the tabs against the crown to stick them.

8 Fit the band **C** onto the crown— it looks neater if the joins in the crown and band align.

9 Apply glue to the tabs on the bottom of the crown and slot through the hole in the brim **D**.

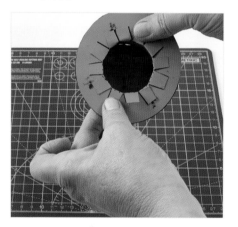

10 Glue the tabs to the bottom of the brim by pulling opposite pairs — this keeps the tension even.

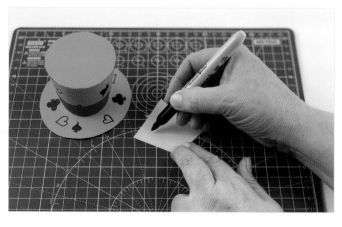

11 Write the name of your guest on the ticket **E**.

12 Tuck the ticket into the brim. Time for tea!

1. Red Riding Hood Lantern

Scan and print these on paper or trace them.
Follow the cut-and-fold instructions exactly.

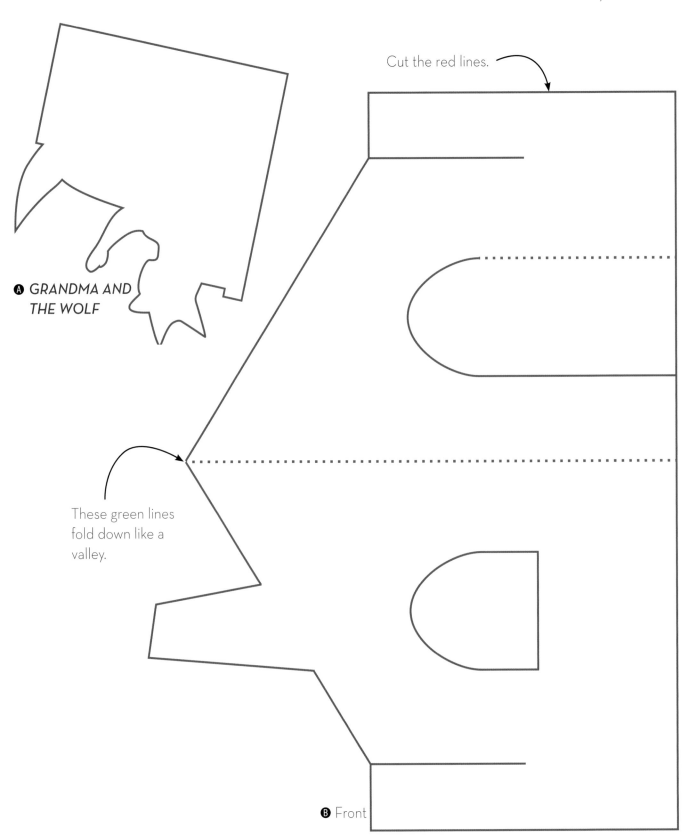

Cut the red lines.

Ⓐ *GRANDMA AND THE WOLF*

These green lines fold down like a valley.

Ⓑ Front

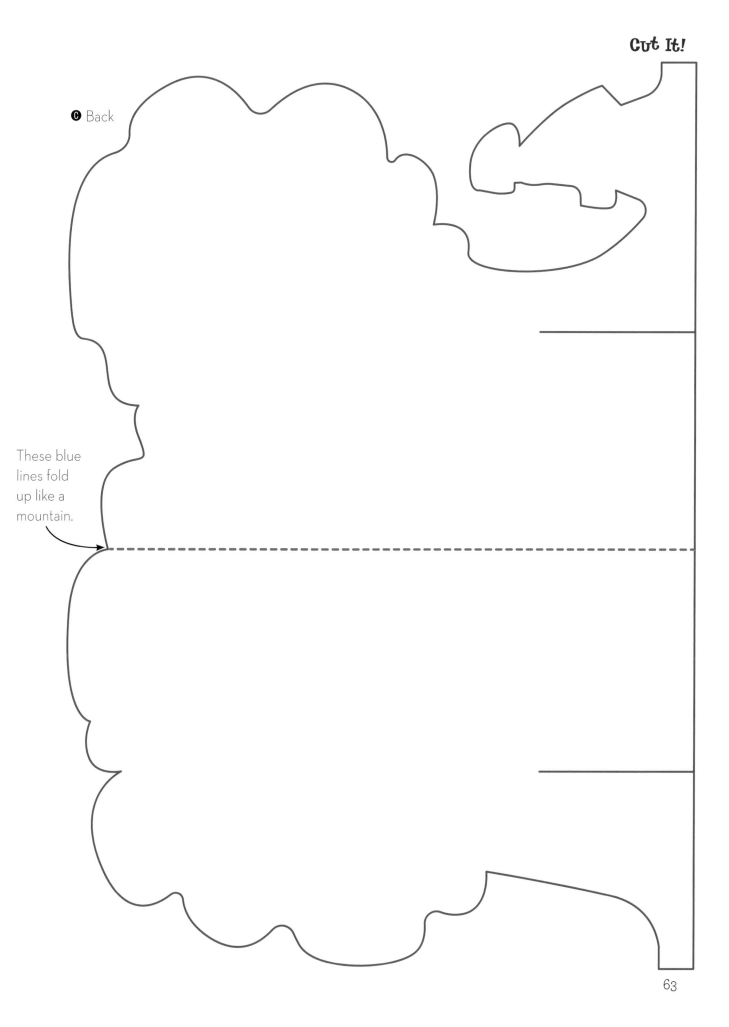

Cut It!

C Back

These blue
lines fold
up like a
mountain.

3. Kraken Lampshade

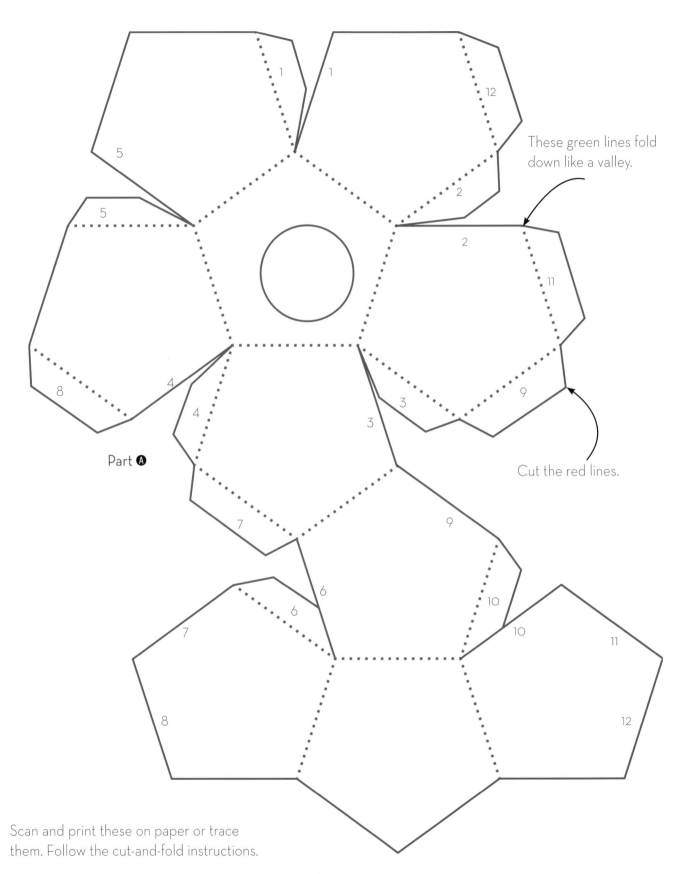

These green lines fold down like a valley.

Cut the red lines.

Part **Ⓐ**

Scan and print these on paper or trace them. Follow the cut-and-fold instructions.

Scan and print two copies of these on paper or trace them. Follow the cut and fold instructions.

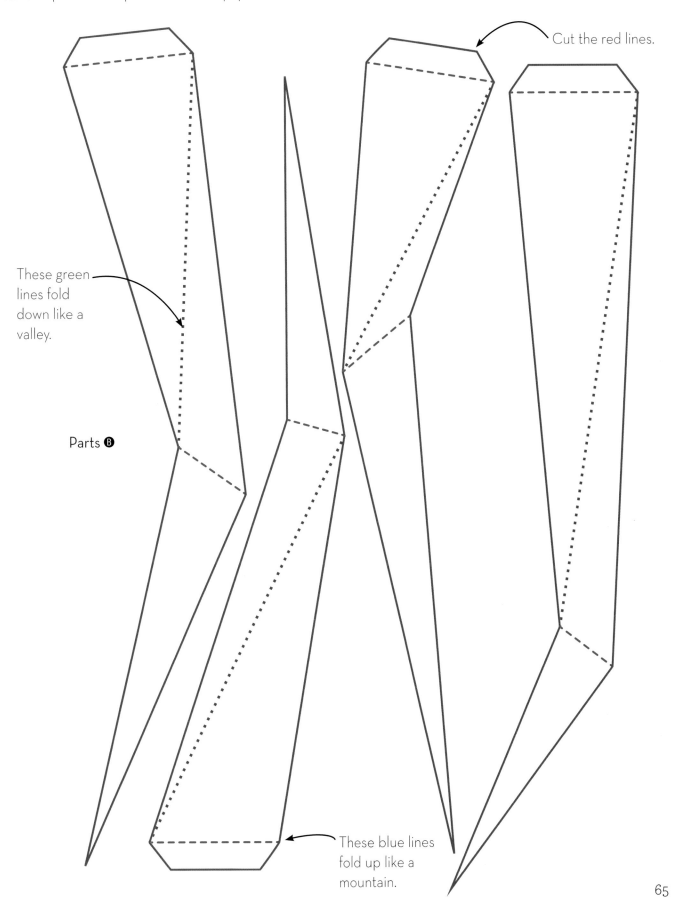

Cut the red lines.

These green lines fold down like a valley.

Parts **B**

These blue lines fold up like a mountain.

4. Sleeping Beauty Mint Tin Diorama

Scan this page and print onto paper.
Follow the cut-and-fold instructions.

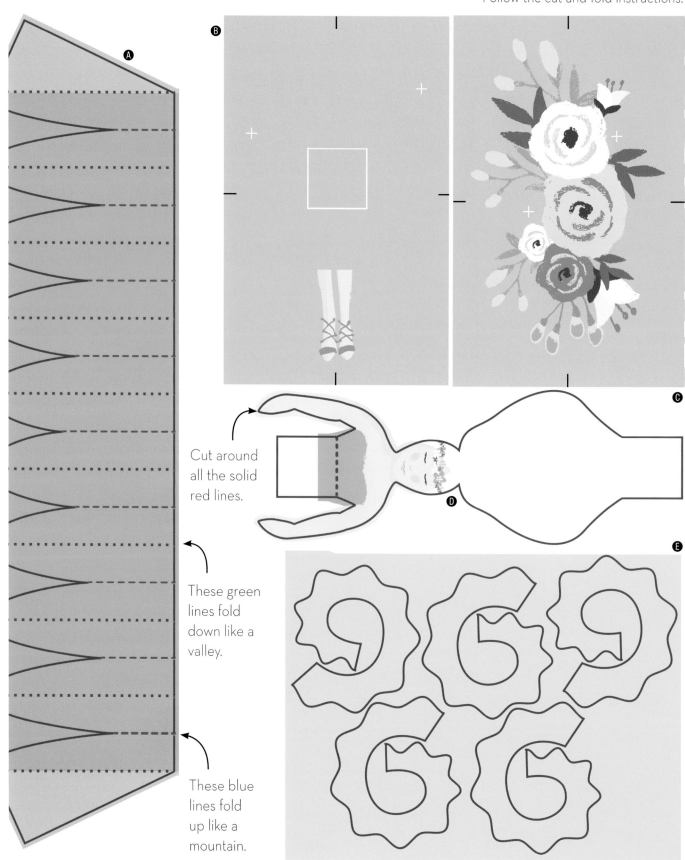

Cut around all the solid red lines.

These green lines fold down like a valley.

These blue lines fold up like a mountain.

5. Paper Bag Forest

Scan and print these on paper or trace them. Follow the cut-and-fold instructions.

Ⓐ Glue to back of base.

Ⓑ

Mountain-fold green lines to form a triangle—this shape makes a good size for a house in the scene.

Base: glue to bottom of the bag.

6. Cake Box Theater

Scan this page and print on to paper.
Follow the cut-and-fold instructions.

Cut out the
red lines.

Cut It!

These blue lines fold up like a mountain.

These green lines fold down like a valley.

8. Robot Puppet

Trace this page onto the **REVERSE** side of your paper. Follow the cut-and-fold instructions.

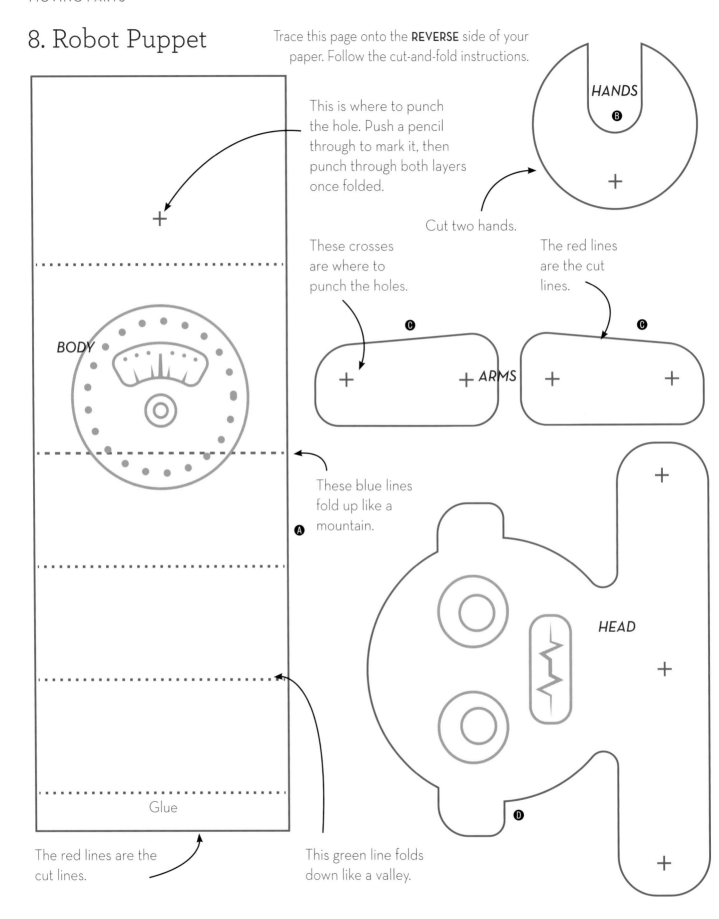

This is where to punch the hole. Push a pencil through to mark it, then punch through both layers once folded.

HANDS

B

Cut two hands.

These crosses are where to punch the holes.

The red lines are the cut lines.

BODY

C

C

ARMS

These blue lines fold up like a mountain.

A

HEAD

Glue

The red lines are the cut lines.

This green line folds down like a valley.

D

13. Pirate Favor Boxes

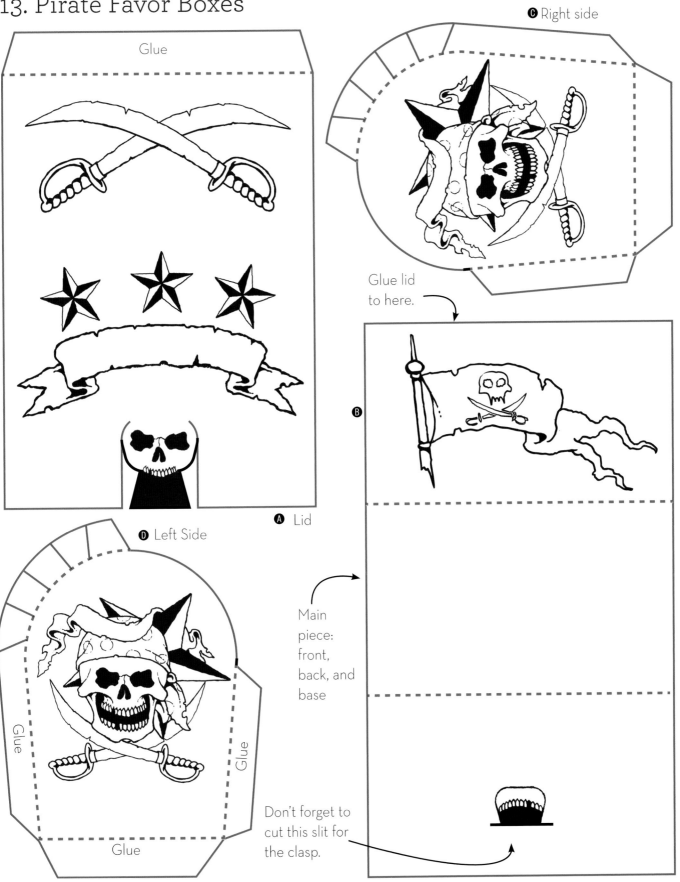

Glue

C Right side

Glue lid to here.

B

A Lid

D Left Side

Glue

Glue

Glue

Main piece: front, back, and base

Don't forget to cut this slit for the clasp.

9. UV Cereal Box Tempest

Trace or print this page onto paper.
Follow the cut-and-fold instructions.

MIDDLE WAVE

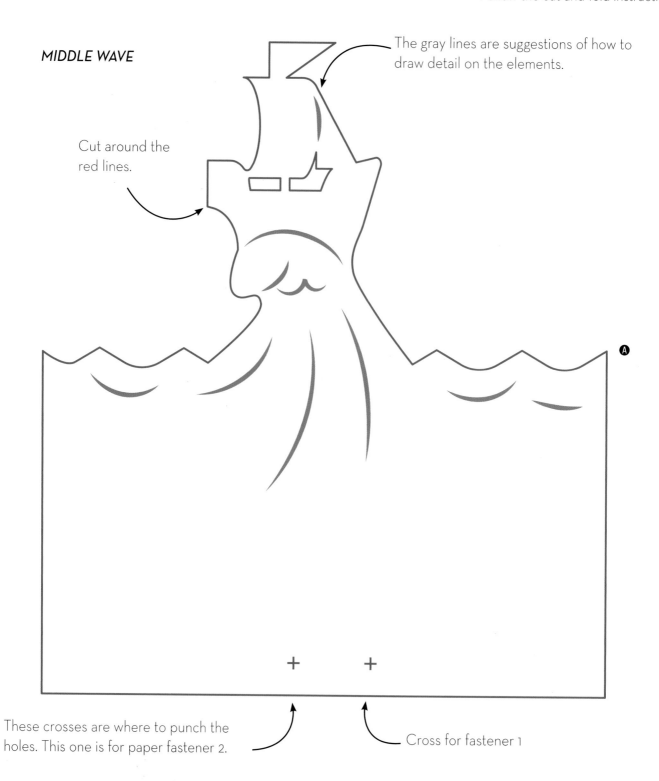

The gray lines are suggestions of how to draw detail on the elements.

Cut around the red lines.

Ⓐ

These crosses are where to punch the holes. This one is for paper fastener 2.

Cross for fastener 1

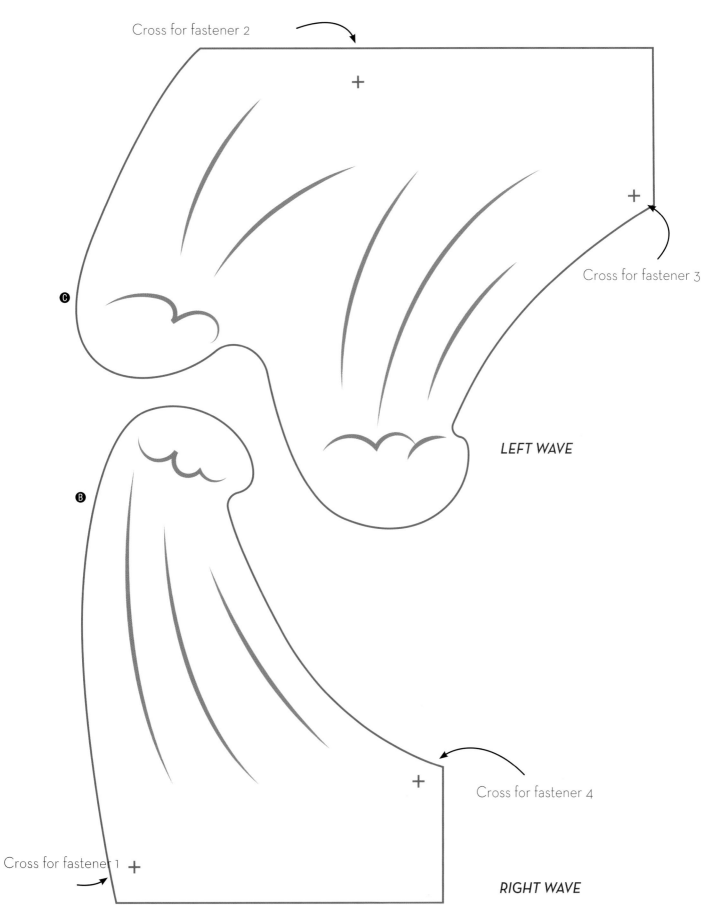

Cross for fastener 2

Cross for fastener 3

G

LEFT WAVE

B

Cross for fastener 4

Cross for fastener 1

RIGHT WAVE

10. A Wolf in Sheep's Clothing

Trace this page onto the **REVERSE** side of your paper.
Follow the cut-and-fold instructions.

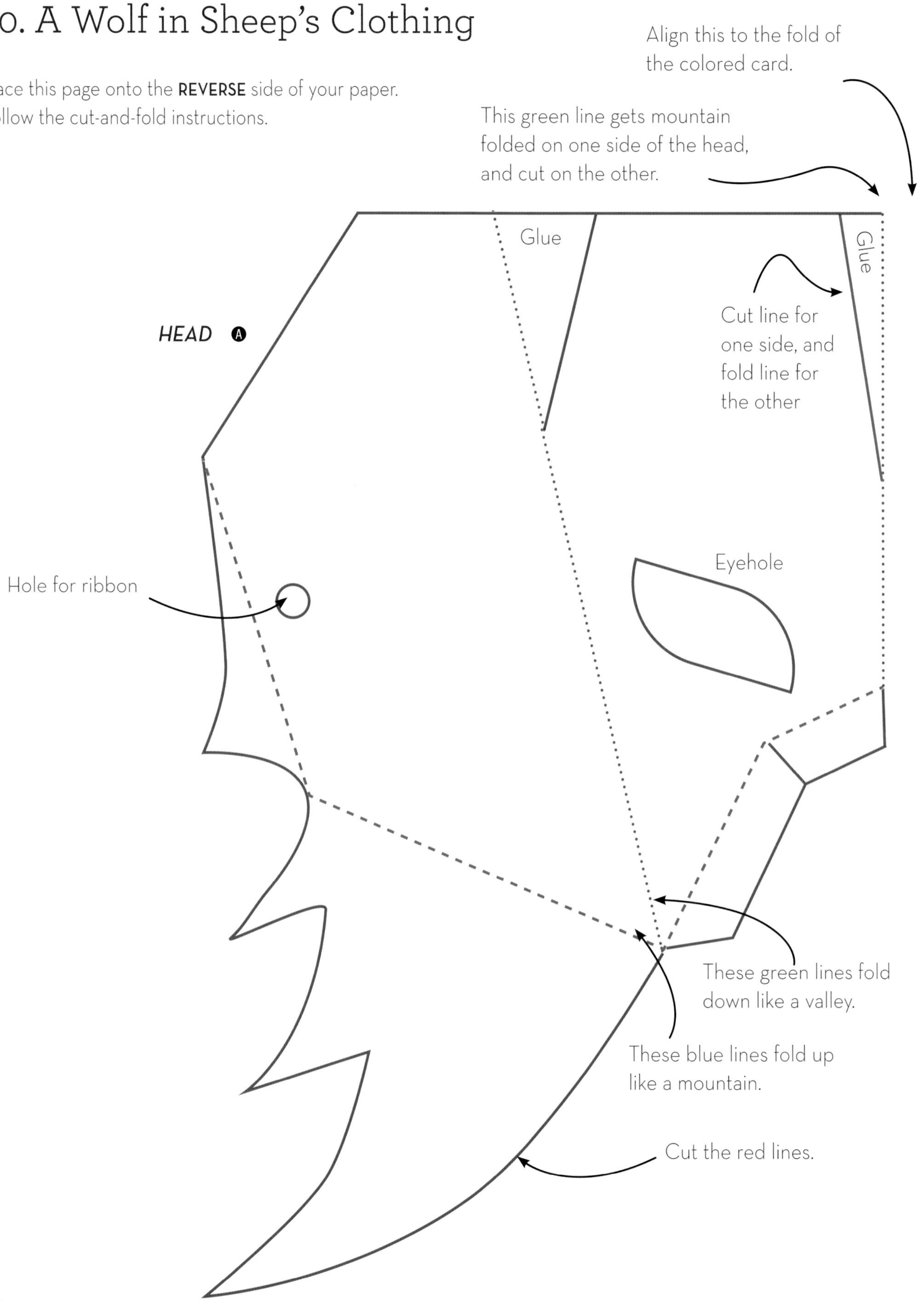

Align this to the fold of
the colored card.

This green line gets mountain
folded on one side of the head,
and cut on the other.

Glue

Glue

HEAD **Ⓐ**

Cut line for
one side, and
fold line for
the other

Eyehole

Hole for ribbon

These green lines fold
down like a valley.

These blue lines fold up
like a mountain.

Cut the red lines.

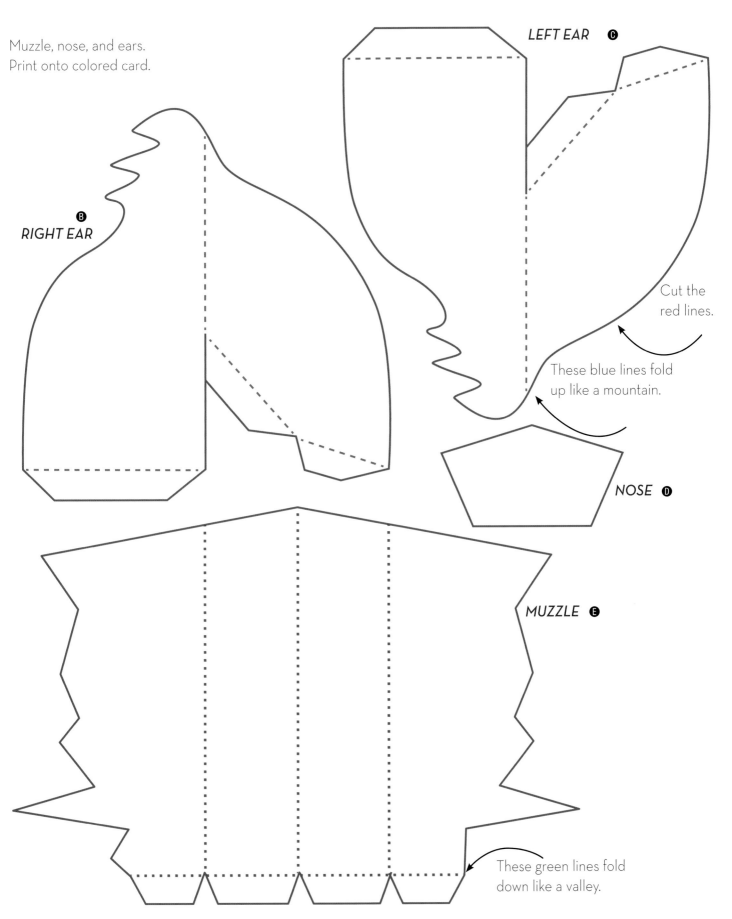

Muzzle, nose, and ears.
Print onto colored card.

RIGHT EAR **Ⓑ**

LEFT EAR **Ⓒ**

Cut the
red lines.

These blue lines fold
up like a mountain.

NOSE **Ⓓ**

MUZZLE **Ⓔ**

These green lines fold
down like a valley.

11. Neptune Mask

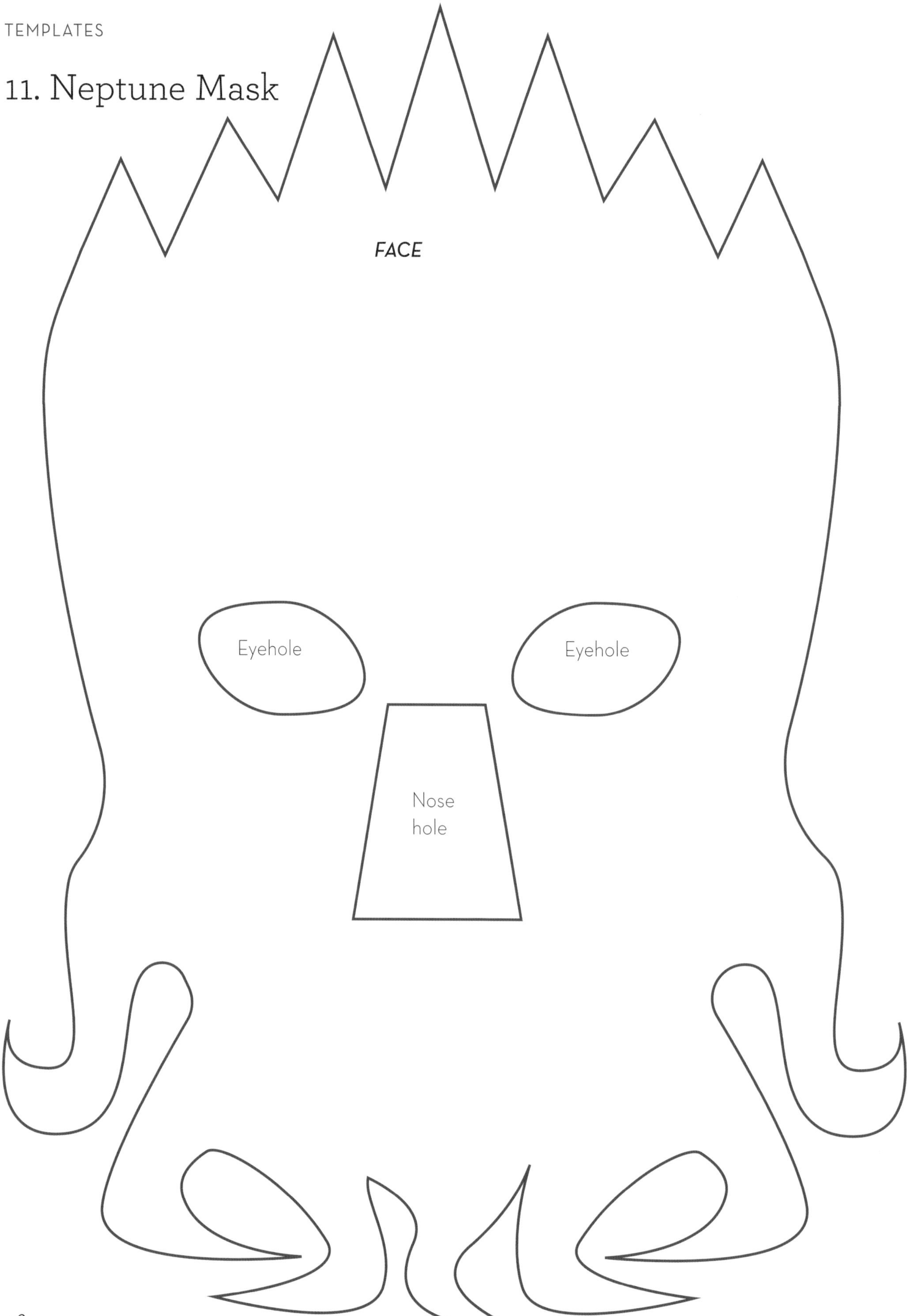

FACE

Eyehole   Eyehole

Nose
hole

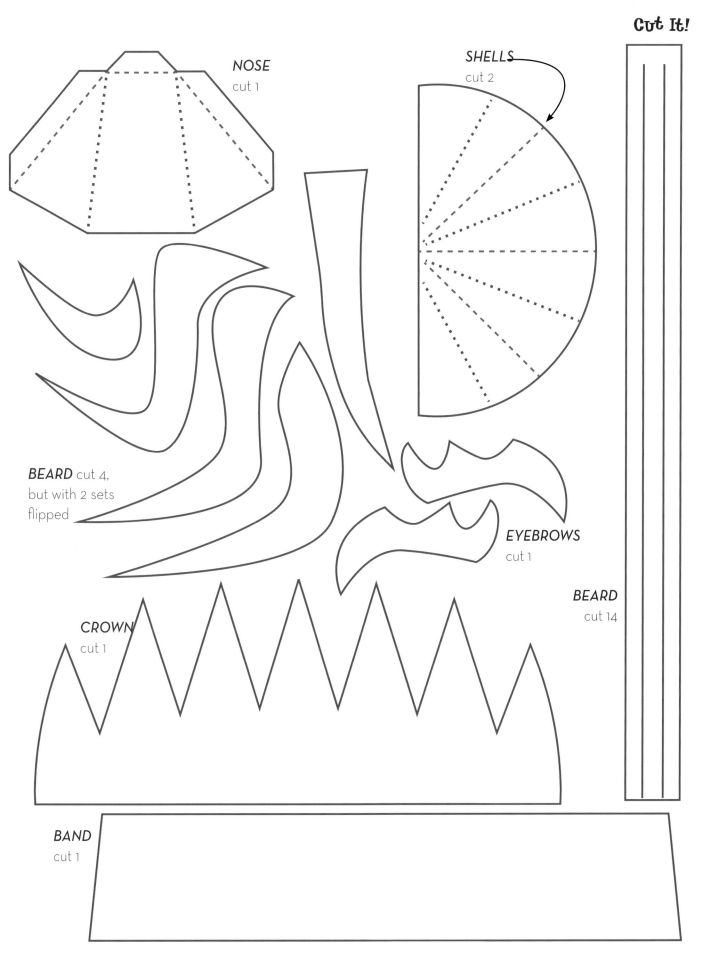

NOSE
cut 1

SHELLS
cut 2

BEARD cut 4,
but with 2 sets
flipped

EYEBROWS
cut 1

BEARD
cut 14

CROWN
cut 1

BAND
cut 1

14. Mexican Halloween Bunting

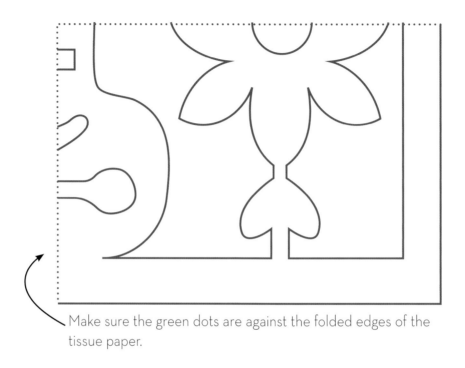

Make sure the green dots are against the folded edges of the tissue paper.

Make sure the green dots are against the folded edges of the tissue paper.

15. Mad Hatter Place Cards

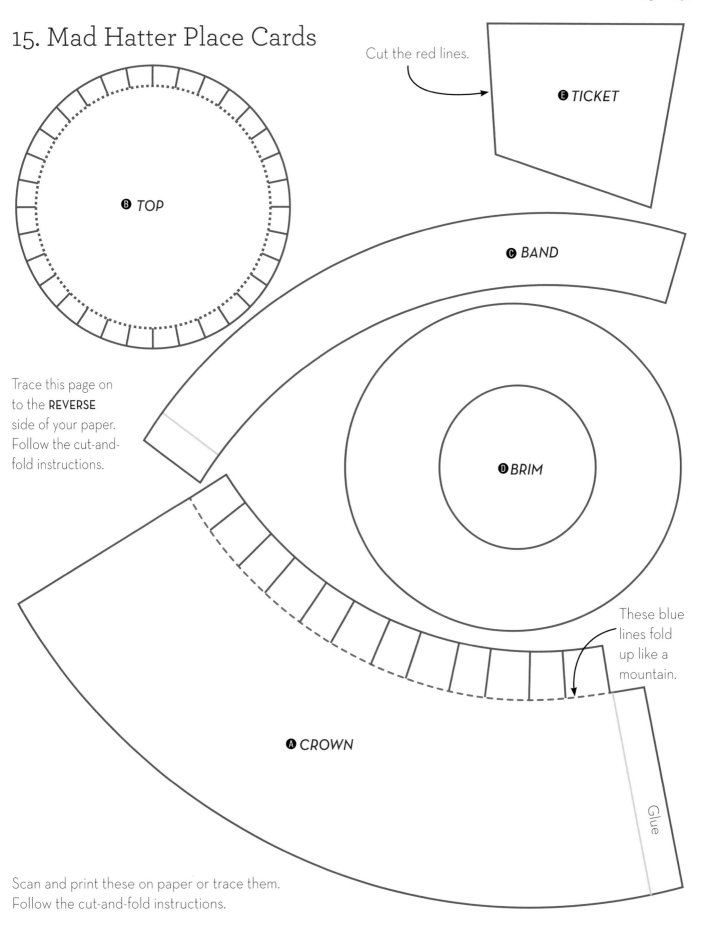

Cut the red lines.

E *TICKET*

B *TOP*

C *BAND*

D *BRIM*

Trace this page on to the **REVERSE** side of your paper. Follow the cut-and-fold instructions.

These blue lines fold up like a mountain.

A *CROWN*

Glue

Scan and print these on paper or trace them. Follow the cut-and-fold instructions.

Acknowledgments

Patterned papers used in Mad Hatter Place Cards:
Retro Feelings Scrapbooking pad by Craft Sensations.

Wolf mask modeled by Ceri Williams.
Venetian mask modeled by Caja Storm.
Neptune mask modeled by Kylan Vaughan.

Sleeping Beauty illustration by Lisa Glanz.

Photography:
Pages 3, 23, 29, 35, 46, and 60 by Adrienne Roisin.
Pages 13, 19, and 55 by Adrienne Roisin, with editing
by the author.
All other photographs by the author.

Locations:
Cardigan Bay and Snowdonia National Park, Wales, UK.
Special thanks to Portmeirion Village for the location for
the Venetian mask photographs.
https://portmeirion.wales

Dedicated to Ela Fach, who is reminding us how important it
is to play.